UNFORGETTABLE DAYS

MONTANA TROUT FISHING

9/13/03
Tight Lines and
Big Trout always
for my fishing
buddy Ed,
Phil

PRECEDING PAGE: *Brown trout, Ruby River*/DENVERBRYAN.COM

Printed in South Korea.

1 2 3 4 5 6 7 8 9 0 SI 07 06 05 04 03 02

Designed by DD Dowden
Edited by Chris Cauble

ISBN I-931832-17-X

Cataloging-in-Publication data is on file at the Library of Congress.

Riverbend Publishing
P.O. Box 5833
Helena, MT 59604
Toll-free I-866-RVR-BEND (787-2363)
Fax I-406-449-0330
www.riverbendpublishing.com

RIVERBEND
PUBLISHING

WORKS & AUTHORS QUOTED

JOE BROOKS

Trout Fishing (1972)

SAM CURTIS

"Fishing for Rumors and Fall Brown Trout,"
Flylines (2001)

GARY FERGUSON

"The Big Hole," *Flylines* (2001)

JOHN GIERACH

Even Brook Trout Get the Blues (1992)
Sex, Death, and Fly-fishing (1990)
Trout Bum (1986)

JIM HARRISON

"A Sporting Life," *Silent Seasons* (1978)

GREG KEELER

"Madison Caddis," *American Falls* (1987)

BUD LILLY

Bud Lilly's Guide to Fly Fishing the New West (2000)

DATUS PROPER

"A Place of our Own," *Flylines* (2001)

ROLAND PERTWEE

"The River God" (1928)

PAUL QUINNETT

Pavlov's Trout (1994)

STEVE SHIMEK

"Lost Fish and Fishermen," *Flylines* (2001)

SCOTT WALDIE

Travers Corners (1997)

ED ZERN

To Hell with Fishing (1945)

DePuy's Spring Creek
DUSANSMETANA.COM

Gallatin River

YOU LOOK DOWN THROUGH THE CLEAR WATER and see every pebble on the bottom and you look up and see the shafts of sunlight through the trees, cathedral-like, heavenly. You hear a splash as a trout rises and you hunch your shoulders and step lightly as you go after him and hold your breath and freeze until you see him rise again. And then you make your cast and see your line laying out, turning over to drop the fly like a feather on the surface, and there he is, and you lightly raise the rod tip and you have him.

These are the rewards of trout fishing. You are far from the grinding clash of traffic, the fumes of civilization. Your mind is completely engrossed in the problem at hand—how to hook that trout. You are far, far away from the tensions of earning a living.

No one has as much fun as a trout fisherman.

JOE BROOKS—*Trout Fishing*

West Gallatin River (LEFT)

Rainbow trout (FAR LEFT)

Madison River (above)

The rise (RIGHT)

Fishing is hope experienced.

Catching a fish is hope affirmed.

A line in the water is hope extended.

Paul Quinnett—*Pavlov's Trout*

Big Hole River

Rainbow trout, Missouri River

Salmonflies

Fly-fishing is a healthy antisocial sport, and many of us have an emotional investment in being misunderstood because it makes us feel strange and brilliant, like Van Gogh.

Maybe that's why, when rumors of a stonefly hatch surface, we have this tendency to drop everything and drive hundreds of miles on the off chance that for once we can catch lots of big trout with almost no effort at all. We've paid our dues, we deserve it and, best of all, there are those who will never understand what all the excitement is about.

Maybe a stonefly hatch changes you and maybe it doesn't. I have noticed that stonefly types have a kind of free-form intensity the rest of us lack: a kind of faith in something beyond reasonable expectations....Like cats, they seem to see something the rest of us don't.

I don't know if it changed A.K. or not, because I met him after he'd hit the stonefly hatch in Montana. I can testify, however, that he's a little crazy now.... Crazy and happy, which is the time-honored posture of the sport.   JOHN GIERACH—*Even Brook Trout Get the Blues*

Brown trout,
salmonfly pattern (RIGHT)

Yellowstone River (FAR RIGHT)

SCOTT SPIKER

Sharing the moment,
Gallatin River (LEFT)

Swiftcurrent Creek (FAR LEFT)

Middle Fork
Flathead River (RIGHT)

Streamside lunch
(FAR RIGHT)

CHRIS CAUBLE

Fishing is the most wonderful thing I do in my life, barring some equally delightful unmentionables, and not disregarding gluttony and booze.

It's in the top five.

JIM HARRISON—*"A Sporting Life"*

Lower Madison River (ABOVE)

Smith River (RIGHT)

Middle Fork
Flathead River
(RIGHT)

Yellowstone River
(FAR RIGHT)

SCOTT SPIKER

Fishermen openly enjoy being thought of as crazy.

John Gierach—*Sex, Death and Fly-fishing*

Avalanche Lake,
Madison Range
(LEFT)

Spring creek,
Gallatin Valley
(FAR LEFT)

Brook trout (ABOVE)

Brown trout (RIGHT)

CHRIS CAUBLE

ONE OF THE FINEST THINGS ABOUT CATCHING A TROUT is being able
to turn it sideways and just look at it. How can so much color
and vibrancy be generated by clear water, gray rocks, and brown bugs?
Trout are among those creatures
who are one hell of a lot prettier
than they need to be.

JOHN GIERACH—*Trout Bum*

Rainbow trout (ABOVE)

Yellowstone River (RIGHT)

Smith River
(RIGHT)

Beaverhead River
(FAR RIGHT)

AL TROTH

Big Hole River (ABOVE)

Rainbow trout (RIGHT)

CHRIS CAUBLE

MANY PEOPLE THINK FISHERMEN ARE *BORN* LIARS.
This is not true. Fishermen *acquire* the talent.

PAUL QUINNETT—*Pavlov's Trout*

FISHERMEN ARE BORN HONEST, but they get over it.

ED ZERN

Rock Creek (ABOVE)

Brown trout, Bighorn River (RIGHT)

HOW BIG A FISH "IS" ASSUMES YOU HAVE THE FISH IN HAND and can measure it. Perish the thought. Nothing shrinks a fish faster than a ruler.

How big a fish "was," on the other hand, allows for all sorts of selective attention and positive distortion. Lost or released fish tend to run bigger than those kept and brought home. At home some depressive can demand that you measure it.

PAUL QUINNETT—*Pavlov's Trout*

AL TROTH

Rainbow trout (ABOVE)

Bighorn River (RIGHT)

DALE C. SPARTAS

T HE FISH JUMPED, SHIMMERING WET SILVER. She was a sight; if she'd been a sound, then the sound would have been thunder.

SCOTT WALDIE—*Travers Corners*

Big Hole River (ABOVE)

Brown trout (RIGHT)

AL TROTH

W E'VE BEEN DOING THIS SINCE THE 14TH CENTURY, for crying
out loud. You'd think we'd be a bit blasé about tossing streamers
and nymphs across autumn waters to goad pugnacious ancestors of Von
Behr and Loch Leven trout. But when daylight shrinks and temperatures
slump, a genetic itch in both brown trout and fly-fishermen begs to be
scratched, right

now and hard.   SAM CURTIS—*"Fishing for Rumors and Fall Brown Trout"*

RICHARD MOUSEL

Goofus Bug (Humpy)
(LEFT)

*Little Prickly
Pear Creek*
(FAR LEFT)

Stanton Lake
(RIGHT)

Lens Lake
(FAR RIGHT)

NEAL MISHLER

I'VE BEEN HERE MANY TIMES BEFORE, but this is my friend Patrick's first trip. I've sworn him to secrecy—he can never divulge specific directions to any of the lakes we will fish.
I'd blindfold him, but the
scenery is just too spectacular.   STEVE SHIMEK—*Lost Fish and Fishermen*

Big Hole River (ABOVE)

Big Hole River (RIGHT)

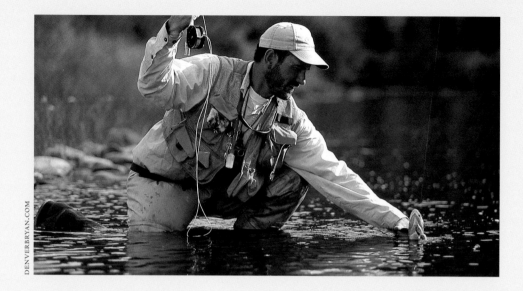

DENVERBRYAN.COM

ALL RIGHT, TRUE BELIEVERS, HERE'S THE DEAL: In the sacred book of the Big Sky, the Big Hole qualifies as a major miracle. We're talking Genesis meets Revelations with a twist of Christmas.

Heaven, the fishermen say, looks an awful lot like the Big Hole.

GARY FERGUSON—*The Big Hole*

Missouri River
(RIGHT)

Rising trout
(FAR RIGHT)

DALE C. SPARTAS

DALE C. SPARTAS

T HE BROWN TROUT AT LEAST HAD THE COURTESY TO FEED

DISCREETLY, but the rainbows got you talking to yourself. They

would lie in mid-stream, taking every

mayfly that came by, except

for the one with a hook in it.

DATUS PROPER—*A Place of Our Own*

Changing flies
(RIGHT)

Heavy artillery
(FAR RIGHT)

I F TROUT HAVE SUCH SMALL BRAINS,
how come they can be so

hard to catch?

PAUL QUINNETT—*Pavlov's Trout*

DALE C. SPARTAS

Centennial Valley (ABOVE)

Yellowstone River (LEFT)

Kootenai River
(RIGHT)

Madison River
(FAR RIGHT)

DALE C. SPARTAS

"WELL, WELL," HE SAID, "please yourself, but isn't it dull not

catching anything?"

And I said, as I've said a thousand

times since, "As if it could be."

ROLAND PERTWEE—*"The River God"*

*Beartooth
Mountains stream*
(RIGHT)

Wood Creek
(FAR RIGHT)

CONRAD ROWE

Madison River (above)

The strike (RIGHT)

As long as I can remember, I was always engaged most by the instant of the strike.

BUD LILLY—*Bud Lilly's Guide to Fly Fishing the New West*

Hook up

I HAVE WONDERED IF IT IS THE WILDNESS IN FISH that somehow renews the wildness in us. After the hook is set and the shiver of something wild comes dancing up the rod, we seem somehow to be released from the confines of our over-civilized selves....

I have seen children squeal, women scream, and men bellow with delight at the first mad run of a just-hooked fish....And in that instant, in that moment of abandonment to pure, uncluttered joy, there is, suddenly and momentarily, a brief glimpse into the untamed, unfettered, wild nature of what man once was, and what he still needs to be from time to time.

PAUL QUINNETT—*Pavlov's Trout*

Caddis hatch (ABOVE)

Caddis hatch, Madison River (RIGHT)

T HEY DRIFT LIKE GLOWING SEEDS

To be planted in those

Quavering pops and circles

There, there, there, and there.

GREG KEELER—*"Madison Caddis"*

Cutthroat trout
(RIGHT)

Paradise Valley lake
(FAR RIGHT)

DALE C. SPARTAS

O F THE MANY SPECIES OF FISH, each has its own special appeal. But none has the universal charisma of trout. Sometimes, as I have fished for other species that I love, I have wondered what lies behind this enchantment with the trout. I believe that it is that, of all fish, the trout demands the most of the angler, and on the angler's meeting of those demands, gives the most in return.

JOE BROOKS—*Trout Fishing*

Rainbow/cutthroat (ABOVE)

Blackfoot River (RIGHT)

Yellowstone River
(RIGHT)

Kootenai River
(FAR RIGHT)

So, I HAVE ASKED MYSELF, "Just what is it we true fishermen are after anyway?"

Dr. Pavlov may have the answer in his freedom reflex and later observations on the nature of wild things. His findings can be briefly summed up as follows:

When trapped or suddenly restricted from natural movement, *all* creatures immediately do two things: struggle to break free, and if able, reorient themselves.

Once free and reoriented, the creature will, in the next split second, make good its escape....

DONALD M. JONES

Rainbow trout, Shields River

... any angler who has freed his quarry after a hard fight has observed what Dr. Pavlov observed. Suddenly released from hook and hand, the fish rests momentarily in the water, righting itself and checking its bearings, and then, *swoosh*, it's gone!

To mirror the fishes we angle for one last time, it seems to me that we all need wildness—deep in our souls, but also at our fingertips. We need ready access to it. We need to be able to touch this wildness, to call it forth when we need it, up and out of the padded cell in which we keep it locked for civilization's sake.

On those days when we feel gang hooked ourselves, and are headed inexorably toward the gaff or landing net, we need to call upon our wildness to struggle to break away, to right ourselves, and to make good our dash for freedom.

PAUL QUINNETT—*Pavlov's Trout*

Yellowstone River